The Relentless Pursuit

Ethel Kennedy's Bold Crusade for Justice and Human Rights

Clever James Publishing

Copyright

All rights reserved. No part of this book may be reproduced, stored in a retrieval system, or transmitted in any form or by any means, electronic, mechanical, photocopying, recording, or otherwise, without the prior written permission of the publisher, except for brief quotations used in reviews.

This book is a work of nonfiction. Any similarity to real persons, living or dead, is coincidental and not intended by the author.

© 2024 by Clever James Publishing

Disclaimer

The content of this book, *The Relentless Pursuit: Ethel Kennedy's Bold Crusade for Justice and Human Rights*, is based on extensive research and publicly available information regarding the life and advocacy work of Ethel Kennedy. While every effort has been made to ensure the accuracy of the facts presented, certain events, interpretations, and conclusions may reflect the author's perspective. The book is intended for informational and educational purposes and is not an official biography or endorsement by Ethel Kennedy, her family, or the Robert F. Kennedy Human Rights organization.

The author and publisher do not assume any legal liability or responsibility for the accuracy, completeness, or usefulness of the information contained herein. Any errors or omissions are unintentional. Readers are encouraged to cross-reference the material with other sources and recognize that human rights advocacy, historical accounts, and personal narratives may evolve over time.

Additionally, this book may reference names, trademarks, and organizations that are the property of their respective owners. These references are used for identification purposes only and do not imply any endorsement, sponsorship, or affiliation with the entities mentioned. The opinions expressed within this book are solely those of the author and do not reflect the views of any individual, group, or organization mentioned herein.

Table Of Contents

Introduction

In a world where the pursuit of justice often feels like a distant ideal, few individuals have stood as relentlessly committed to human rights as Ethel Kennedy. As the widow of Senator Robert F. Kennedy, Ethel could have easily been relegated to a footnote in history—a tragic figure marked by loss. Instead, she emerged as a towering force in her own right, driven by a fierce determination to carry forward her late husband's vision of a more just and equitable world. But her journey is not merely an extension of his legacy; it is a story of a woman who found her own voice and transformed personal tragedy into a lifelong mission for social change.

The Relentless Pursuit: Ethel Kennedy's Bold Crusade for Justice and Human Rights chronicles Ethel's remarkable contributions to global human rights advocacy. From standing against apartheid in South Africa to supporting civil rights movements in the United States, her fight was not bound by borders. Through the Robert F. Kennedy Human Rights organization, she built an enduring platform that continues to champion the rights of the oppressed and marginalized across the globe. This book delves deep into her transformative impact, exploring her most notable campaigns, the legal battles she waged, and the many lives she has touched along the way.

This is the story of an unwavering woman whose resilience, courage, and compassion reshaped the landscape of human rights advocacy. It is a testament to how one individual can galvanize others and change the course of history—not only by standing up to injustice but by inspiring future generations to do the same. Ethel Kennedy's legacy is a living, breathing force that continues to echo in the corridors of power and the streets where ordinary people fight for their dignity every day. This book aims to capture the essence of that legacy, inviting readers to walk alongside her as she forged an extraordinary path

in the relentless pursuit of justice.

Chapter One

The Early Years: Seeds of Activism

Ethel Skakel Kennedy's story is one marked by a unique combination of privilege, tragedy, and an unyielding sense of responsibility. Born into one of America's wealthiest families on April 11, 1928, Ethel's early years laid the foundation for a life dedicated to social justice and human rights. Her father, George Skakel, was a self-made millionaire, having built a fortune in the coal industry, and her mother, Ann Brannack Skakel, was a devout Catholic. Ethel grew up in a household that embodied the values of faith, hard work, and service to others—principles that would shape her future endeavors. Yet, it was the complex interplay of these early influences and the world she would eventually step into through her marriage to Robert F. Kennedy that propelled her into a relentless pursuit of justice, advocating for those who could not speak for themselves.

Ethel's upbringing in Greenwich, Connecticut, was a privileged one, but it was not without challenges. The Skakels were one of the wealthiest families in their affluent neighborhood, living in a sprawling 31-room mansion. But despite the material wealth, Ethel's parents instilled in their children the importance of humility and the Catholic faith's emphasis on service to the less fortunate. The Skakels were devout Catholics, and their faith was central to their lives. Ethel attended the all-girls Greenwich Academy and later the Convent of the Sacred Heart in Manhattan, prestigious institutions that reinforced her religious upbringing while exposing her to a rigorous education. The nuns at Sacred Heart emphasized moral duty, and it was there that Ethel first encountered the idea that those who have been blessed with much are expected to give back in equal measure.

Ethel was not the quiet, demure young woman of her era. Even as a child, she displayed a fiery and independent spirit. She was adventurous, athletic, and, by many accounts, had a mischievous streak. This set her apart from the conventional expectations of women in the 1930s and 1940s. She enjoyed sports and excelled in tennis, swimming, and horseback riding—activities that were traditionally reserved for boys. But Ethel's tomboyish nature did not diminish her sense of compassion. Those close to her recall that she always had an interest in helping others, particularly those who were less fortunate. In many ways, Ethel's early years set the stage for her future role as a fearless advocate for justice, a role she would embrace fully after stepping into the Kennedy family's world.

It was during her time at Manhattanville College of the Sacred Heart in New York that Ethel's life took a significant turn. She became close friends with Jean Kennedy, the younger sister of Robert F. Kennedy, whom she would later marry. The Kennedy family's deep involvement in politics and public service would have a profound influence on Ethel, shaping her understanding of the power of political action to create change. The Kennedy family was not only politically powerful but also deeply committed to the Catholic principle of social justice, a value that resonated with Ethel's upbringing. The

Kennedys were known for their sense of public duty, their belief in using their power and privilege to uplift others. This sense of duty, coupled with the family's political influence, had a magnetic pull on Ethel.

In 1950, Ethel met Robert F. Kennedy while on a ski trip. The two quickly became inseparable, bonding over their shared love of sports, adventure, and a commitment to Catholic values. They married on June 17, 1950, and Ethel was thrust into the heart of one of America's most prominent political families. But Ethel was not content to simply be a political wife. From the beginning of her marriage, she was an active partner in Robert's political career, encouraging him to take bold stances on issues of social justice and human rights. Ethel's influence on Robert cannot be overstated. While Robert came from a family steeped in politics, it was Ethel who pushed him to consider the broader implications of social injustice and to fight for the underprivileged, even when it was not politically expedient.

As Robert Kennedy rose through the ranks of American politics, first as a lawyer, then as Attorney General, and later as a U.S. Senator, Ethel was by his side, not just as a supportive spouse, but as an integral part of his political machine. The couple's home in McLean, Virginia, became known for its open-door policy, where activists, politicians, and civil rights leaders were always welcome. Ethel's presence in these spaces was not that of a passive observer. She engaged in discussions about civil rights, poverty, and justice with the same fervor as her husband. In many ways, Ethel was the moral compass of the Kennedy operation, consistently pushing Robert to take stands on the most pressing social issues of the day, including the Civil Rights Movement, which was rapidly gaining momentum during the 1960s.

The assassination of John F. Kennedy in 1963 was a pivotal moment for Ethel and the entire Kennedy family. The loss was devastating, but it also galvanized the family's sense of duty to continue John's legacy of social reform. Robert, in particular, was deeply affected by his brother's death and began to shift his focus from law enforcement to social justice, a transformation that Ethel played a key role in shaping. Her tireless work behind the scenes, her constant encouragement, and her unwavering belief in Robert's ability to affect change, were instrumental in his decision to run for the U.S. Senate and later for the presidency.

Ethel's passion for justice was not confined to the domestic sphere. She became increasingly interested in international human rights, particularly in Latin America and Africa. Ethel recognized that the fight for justice could not be limited to the United States; it was a global struggle. She and Robert visited several countries during his tenure as Attorney General and later as a senator, meeting with local leaders and activists fighting for freedom and equality. Ethel was particularly moved by the plight of those living under oppressive regimes, and she began to see human rights advocacy as an essential component of her work. Her exposure to global issues during these trips fueled her determination to make human rights a central part of Robert's political platform.

Throughout the 1960s, Ethel's commitment to justice grew, as did her family. The Kennedys had eleven children together, and despite the demands of raising a large family, Ethel remained deeply involved in her husband's work. She often traveled with him on political campaigns, using her platform to speak out on issues of poverty, civil rights, and human dignity. She was not content to sit in the background; Ethel wanted to be part of the action. Her speeches during Robert's Senate and presidential campaigns were passionate calls for justice, particularly for the poor and disenfranchised. Her commitment to these causes was not just political; it was deeply personal. Ethel believed that those with privilege had a moral obligation to use their influence to fight for those without it.

Ethel's life took another tragic turn on June 5, 1968, when Robert Kennedy was assassinated while campaigning for the presidency. Once again, Ethel found herself in the role of a widow, this time with the immense responsibility of raising eleven children on her own. But even in the face of unimaginable grief, Ethel's commitment to justice did not waver. In the wake of Robert's death, she founded the Robert F. Kennedy Memorial, now known as RFK Human Rights, an organization dedicated to continuing her husband's work on behalf of the world's most vulnerable populations.

Chapter Two

The Awakening: Ethel's Path to Justice

Ethel Kennedy's life took a sharp and irreversible turn after the tragic assassination of her husband, Robert F. Kennedy, in 1968. Once a vibrant presence beside her charismatic husband during his campaign for social justice and political reform, Ethel was thrust into a different role—one of solitary determination and personal transformation. The world knew her as the supportive wife of a man who had dedicated his life to making America a more equitable society, but Robert's death ignited something even deeper within her. It was in the wake of profound grief that Ethel Kennedy began to emerge as a formidable advocate in her own right, one whose passion for justice became a defining feature of her public life.

Before Robert's death, Ethel was deeply involved in the behind-the-scenes aspects of political life, raising her children and supporting her husband's career. Their home was a gathering place for political allies, artists, intellectuals, and anyone committed to the cause of social progress. Ethel had always championed the underdog, but it was her husband's assassination that propelled her into a new realm of activism. No longer was she just the woman standing beside a man of great influence—she was becoming a figure of power and resilience herself, channeling her personal tragedy into a greater cause.

The transformation from grieving widow to justice advocate did not happen overnight. Ethel faced an uphill battle against societal expectations. Many believed her role should be confined to raising her 11 children and maintaining the Kennedy legacy privately. But for Ethel, the greatest tribute to her husband was not only continuing his work but expanding its scope to touch the lives of people around the world. Robert's vision of a better America became her guiding star, and she knew that her voice could amplify those values in ways that went beyond politics. It was about justice, equality, and the rights of all human beings.

One of the earliest signs of this shift in Ethel's public life came shortly after Robert's death when she threw herself into supporting political candidates who shared her late husband's values.

She campaigned for figures like George McGovern, who advocated for civil rights and opposed the Vietnam War. Ethel's energy and commitment to justice transcended party lines—she was more interested in pushing forward the ideals that Robert had championed than adhering to partisan politics. This commitment would become a hallmark of her activism as she transitioned into the realm of human rights advocacy.

Though politics remained close to her heart, Ethel's attention began to shift to issues that resonated on a global scale. The assassination of Robert Kennedy had awakened in her a profound sense of urgency for the oppressed, the marginalized, and the voiceless. She saw injustice not just in America, but all over the world. Her worldview, once rooted in national politics, expanded to a global landscape where the fight for human rights became a central focus. It was during this time that she began to lay the foundation for the creation of the Robert F. Kennedy Human Rights Foundation, an organization dedicated to continuing Robert's legacy of justice through activism, litigation, and education. Ethel's vision was to not only honor her husband's memory but to create real, tangible change.

Ethel's efforts were not limited to political maneuvering. She became an outspoken critic of regimes and systems that oppressed people, particularly those in underdeveloped countries where human rights abuses were rampant. She didn't just advocate from afar; Ethel traveled the world, meeting with activists, victims of injustice, and political prisoners. Her physical presence in places where human rights were being violated signaled her deep commitment to these causes. Whether it was the plight of political prisoners in apartheid-era South Africa or the injustices faced by indigenous people in Latin America, Ethel used her platform to shed light on the darkest corners of human suffering.

She had a unique ability to blend her privilege and access to power with grassroots activism. Despite her status as a Kennedy, she was not removed from the struggles of everyday people. In fact, she made it her mission to be deeply embedded in these causes, understanding the stories of those who suffered firsthand. Her approach was deeply personal—she wasn't just raising awareness; she was standing in solidarity with the oppressed. This personal connection to the fight for justice made her advocacy all the more powerful. She could easily command the attention of world leaders, but her heart was with the people on the ground.

As the 1970s progressed, Ethel's activism took on a sharper, more defined focus. She started to champion causes that weren't necessarily popular or politically expedient. For example, she became a vocal opponent of the death penalty, even in cases where public opinion was overwhelmingly in favor of capital punishment. She argued that the state should not have the power to take a life, no matter the crime. Her stance on the death penalty put her at odds with many political allies, but it was consistent with her deep belief in the sanctity of human life and the power of redemption.

Ethel also became involved in advocating for those wrongfully imprisoned, particularly political dissidents and prisoners of conscience. She worked closely with organizations like Amnesty International, using her influence to bring attention to cases that would have otherwise been ignored. She didn't just write letters or attend meetings—she visited prisons, spoke to the families of prisoners, and publicly called for their release. Ethel was relentless in her pursuit of justice for these individuals, and her efforts were instrumental in securing freedom for many.

Her passion for justice was not confined to any single cause; it was part of a broader philosophy that saw the interconnectedness of all human rights issues. Whether it was racial injustice, economic inequality, or gender discrimination,

Ethel viewed these struggles as part of the same fight for a fairer, more just world. This holistic view of justice set her apart from many of her contemporaries, who often focused on specific issues in isolation. For Ethel, justice was universal, and it was something worth fighting for in every corner of the globe.

The creation of the RFK Human Rights Foundation was the culmination of Ethel's transformation from political spouse to human rights crusader. The foundation, which she led with fierce dedication, became a powerful force for change. It provided legal and financial support for activists, funded educational programs, and offered a platform for those fighting injustice around the world. Under her leadership, the foundation tackled issues ranging from poverty to political repression, always with the same goal: to promote justice and human dignity.

Ethel Kennedy's journey into activism is a testament to her resilience and determination. The assassination of Robert Kennedy could have marked the end of her public life, but instead, it sparked a new beginning. Her transformation from a grieving widow into a fierce advocate for justice is one of the most remarkable stories of personal reinvention in modern history. Through her relentless pursuit of justice, Ethel Kennedy has not only honored her husband's legacy but has carved out her own place in the pantheon of human rights advocates.

Chapter Three

Championing Human Rights: A New Frontline

Ethel Kennedy's journey into human rights advocacy was not a premeditated path but one born out of personal tragedy and moral conviction. Following the assassination of her husband, Robert F. Kennedy, Ethel could have easily retreated into the shadow of mourning, choosing a quieter life focused on family. But Ethel Kennedy was never one to be passive. Instead, she stepped into the public arena, determined to champion the causes her husband cared deeply about, while also expanding her scope to global human rights issues that had not always been front and center of the American political consciousness.

One of Ethel's defining characteristics has been her steadfast determination. In the wake of Bobby's death, she emerged as a fierce advocate for justice, not only within the United States but across the world. At a time when international human rights were often seen as separate from American domestic policy, Ethel Kennedy made it clear that injustice anywhere was a threat to justice everywhere. Her work has spanned continents, touching issues ranging from political repression in Latin America to the struggles for racial equality in South Africa, to poverty and hunger in Africa, and beyond.

A key component of Ethel's advocacy has been her ability to humanize the stories of those who have been oppressed. She has long believed in the power of personal stories to bring about change, and this has been a hallmark of her work. Ethel's efforts were not limited to issuing statements or attending conferences. She went into the field, meeting with victims of oppression and standing with them as a visible symbol of solidarity. By doing so, she helped to shed light on human rights violations that may have otherwise been ignored by the Western media. Ethel's visibility as a Kennedy was a powerful tool, but it was her empathy and unyielding commitment that truly made her an effective advocate.

Latin America was one of the first regions where Ethel Kennedy made her mark as a human rights advocate. In the 1970s and 1980s, many countries in the region were ruled by military dictatorships, regimes that silenced dissent through brutal means, including torture, disappearances, and extrajudicial killings. Ethel was one of the first prominent American figures to publicly denounce these regimes, calling attention to the human cost of the political repression that swept through the region. She worked alongside organizations such as Amnesty International and the RFK Human Rights Foundation to bring international pressure on these dictatorships. Her efforts helped to bring about some reforms and, in some cases, the release of political prisoners. But more importantly, her involvement helped to elevate the stories of the victims, ensuring that their suffering was not forgotten by the global community.

One of the most significant human rights issues that Ethel Kennedy engaged with during this period was the fight against apartheid in South Africa. Like her husband before her, Ethel was a staunch opponent of racial segregation and discrimination. Apartheid, the system of institutionalized racial discrimination in South Africa, represented everything she stood against. Ethel became a vocal advocate for the anti-apartheid movement, lending her support to Nelson Mandela and other leaders who were fighting to dismantle this unjust system. At a time when many political figures were hesitant to take a strong stance on apartheid for fear of political backlash, Ethel Kennedy's unwavering commitment to the cause set her apart. She used her platform to raise awareness about the suffering of Black South Africans and called for economic sanctions against the South African government, a controversial stance at the time but one that ultimately played a role in bringing about the end of apartheid.

Beyond political repression, Ethel Kennedy also tackled issues of poverty, hunger, and access to education. She understood that human rights were not just about freedom from political oppression, but also about ensuring that every person had the opportunity to live a life of dignity. This is perhaps best exemplified by her work in Africa, where she traveled extensively to raise awareness about the ongoing humanitarian crises affecting millions of people. In many ways, Ethel's advocacy in Africa was an extension of her late husband's commitment to addressing the root causes of poverty and inequality. She focused on highlighting the ways in which global economic policies, often driven by Western nations, were contributing to the suffering of people in developing countries. She advocated for fair trade policies, debt relief for impoverished nations, and increased international aid to address the basic needs of food, water, and education.

Ethel Kennedy's approach to human rights advocacy was holistic. She understood that systemic issues like poverty and political repression were interconnected and that lasting change required a multifaceted approach. One of the ways she sought to address this was through her involvement with the Robert F. Kennedy Human Rights Foundation, which she helped to establish in 1968. Under her leadership, the foundation became a leading voice in the global human rights movement. It not only advocated for political prisoners and victims of repression but also worked to promote economic and social justice through initiatives aimed at empowering marginalized communities.

A key aspect of the foundation's work under Ethel's guidance was its focus on youth and education. Ethel believed that the fight for human rights could not be won without engaging the next generation. She championed programs that aimed to inspire young people to become advocates for change in their own communities. This focus on youth was particularly evident in the RFK Speak Truth to Power program, which educates students about human rights issues and encourages them to become active participants in the global fight for justice. Through this program and others, Ethel has ensured that her husband's legacy of fighting for the underprivileged continues to inspire future generations.

Ethel's work was not without its challenges. Advocating for human rights on a global scale often meant going up against powerful interests, both in the United States and abroad. Many of the regimes and institutions she challenged had the backing of Western governments, and Ethel faced criticism for her outspokenness. But she remained undeterred. For her, the fight for justice was not about political expediency or personal gain. It was about standing up for what was right, even when it was difficult or unpopular. This is perhaps what has made Ethel Kennedy such an enduring figure in the human rights movement. She has never wavered in her commitment to the cause, even in the face of personal loss and political opposition.

One of the most significant aspects of Ethel Kennedy's advocacy has been her ability to bridge the gap between high-level policy discussions and grassroots activism. She has always believed that true change comes from the bottom up and that the voices of the oppressed must be heard if justice is to be achieved. This is why, even as she engaged with world leaders and policymakers, Ethel remained committed to working with local human rights activists and community leaders. She understood that they were the ones who were truly on the frontlines of the fight for justice, and she sought to amplify their voices and support their work in any way she could.

Over the decades, Ethel Kennedy's work has had a profound impact on the global human rights movement. Through her advocacy, she has helped to bring attention to some of the most pressing human rights issues of our time, from political repression to poverty and hunger. She has inspired countless others to join the fight for justice, including many members of her own family, who have carried on the Kennedy legacy of public service and activism. Her work has not only honored the memory of her late husband but has also left an indelible mark on the world, reminding us all of the power of one person to make a difference.

Chapter Four

The Founding of RFK Human Rights

In the wake of Robert F. Kennedy's tragic assassination in 1968, the world witnessed not just the loss of a promising political leader, but the birth of a legacy that would shape the global fight for human rights for generations. At the heart of this legacy stood Ethel Kennedy, a woman who refused to be defined by grief or relegated to the background of history. Instead, she transformed her sorrow into a driving force for justice, establishing the Robert F. Kennedy Human Rights organization in 1968. This organization became the vessel through which she channeled the ideals that her late husband had championed, offering a beacon of hope for the oppressed and marginalized around the world.

In the years that followed Robert Kennedy's death, Ethel Kennedy was faced with the monumental task of carrying on his mission. Robert had been a tireless advocate for civil rights, social justice, and equality, and his vision for a better, fairer world was one that Ethel had not only supported but had lived alongside him. She knew that the work could not end with his passing. She had seen firsthand the transformative power of human rights advocacy through her husband's campaigns, and she was determined to honor his memory by ensuring that the principles he stood for would continue to resonate in the lives of those most in need. Thus, the Robert F. Kennedy Human Rights organization was born, rooted in the principles of courage, justice, and equality.

Ethel's decision to found the organization was not merely a gesture of remembrance; it was a bold declaration that the fight for justice was far from over. The political and social landscape of the late 1960s was fraught with unrest—civil rights movements were gaining momentum, anti-war protests were raging across the country, and injustices around the world were coming to light. It was in this context that Ethel envisioned the RFK Human Rights organization as a vehicle for global change, an organization that would take on the most pressing human rights issues of the time and beyond. She saw it not only as a means to honor her husband's legacy but as a continuation of his life's work, adapted to the changing dynamics of the world.

From its inception, the RFK Human Rights organization positioned itself at the forefront of some of the most critical social justice battles of the 20th century. Its mission was clear: to support human rights defenders and activists worldwide, to challenge oppressive regimes, and to promote justice where it was most needed. But the organization was not just about addressing immediate crises; it also sought to build sustainable movements for change by fostering the next generation of human rights advocates. Ethel Kennedy understood that the struggle for justice required not just swift responses to current abuses but also a long-term strategy that empowered individuals and communities to stand up for their rights.

One of the early hallmarks of the RFK Human Rights organization was its commitment to spotlighting the stories of those who were often overlooked by the media and political systems. Ethel Kennedy and her team believed that by amplifying the voices of the marginalized, they could draw global attention to injustices that might otherwise go unnoticed. This approach was instrumental in shaping the organization's activities, from their support of dissidents in authoritarian countries to their efforts to expose the abuses faced by indigenous peoples and other vulnerable populations. Ethel believed in the power of storytelling, recognizing that personal narratives of suffering and resilience had the potential to mobilize public opinion and catalyze change.

A critical component of the organization's early work was the establishment of the Robert F. Kennedy Human Rights Award. This prestigious honor was designed to recognize individuals who had demonstrated extraordinary courage and commitment in the face of human rights abuses. Ethel wanted the award to serve as both a tribute to her late husband's ideals and as a platform for the awardees to gain international recognition for their efforts. Through the award, the organization was able to bring attention to the work of human rights defenders from around the globe, many of whom operated in dangerous and repressive environments. The recipients of the RFK Human Rights Award were not just celebrated for their achievements; they were also provided with financial and logistical support, helping them to continue their vital work in the face of adversity.

The RFK Human Rights organization quickly expanded its reach, taking on high-profile causes and working alongside international organizations and governments to address systemic abuses. One of the areas where the organization had a profound impact was in the fight against apartheid in South Africa. Ethel Kennedy was an outspoken critic of the South African government's policies of racial segregation and discrimination, and the RFK Human Rights organization played a key role in supporting the anti-apartheid movement. The organization worked to raise awareness about the plight of black South Africans, mobilizing support for economic sanctions and political pressure that ultimately contributed to the dismantling of apartheid.

Beyond its work in South Africa, the RFK Human Rights organization was deeply involved in efforts to combat poverty and inequality around the world. Ethel Kennedy saw poverty as one of the greatest human rights challenges of her time, understanding that economic injustice was often at the root of other forms of oppression. Under her leadership, the organization launched numerous initiatives aimed at addressing the root causes of poverty, including education programs, microfinance projects, and advocacy for fair labor practices. Ethel believed that empowering communities economically was a fundamental step toward ensuring that all individuals could enjoy their basic human rights.

One of the defining features of Ethel Kennedy's approach to human rights advocacy was her unwavering optimism. Despite the enormity of the challenges she and her organization faced, Ethel remained steadfast in her belief that change was possible. This optimism was contagious, inspiring those around her to remain committed to the cause even in the face of setbacks. Her leadership style was one of quiet determination—she was not one for grandstanding or seeking the spotlight, but her presence was felt in every aspect of the organization's work. Ethel's ability to inspire others, both within the RFK Human Rights organization and beyond, was one of her greatest strengths as a leader.

In addition to its international work, the RFK Human Rights organization was also deeply involved in domestic issues within the United States. Ethel Kennedy was a passionate advocate for civil rights and social justice at home, and the organization played a key role in supporting movements for racial equality, LGBTQ+ rights, and criminal justice reform. One of the organization's landmark initiatives was its partnership with the Innocence Project, which sought to exonerate wrongfully convicted individuals and reform the criminal justice system to prevent such injustices from occurring in the future. Through its work with the Innocence Project, the RFK Human Rights organization helped to secure the release of numerous individuals who had been imprisoned for crimes they did not commit, shining a light on the flaws in the American legal system.

As the years passed, the RFK Human Rights organization continued to evolve, adapting its strategies to address the changing landscape of global human rights. Under Ethel's guidance, the organization remained nimble and responsive to new challenges, from the rise of authoritarianism to the impacts of climate change on vulnerable communities. Ethel understood that the fight for justice was a dynamic and ever-evolving struggle, and she was committed to ensuring that the RFK Human Rights organization would remain at the forefront of that fight for as long as it was needed.

Throughout her life, Ethel Kennedy has been a tireless advocate for human rights, and the RFK Human Rights organization stands as a testament to her enduring commitment to justice. The organization's work has touched countless lives around the world, providing hope to those who have been silenced and empowering them to demand their rights. Ethel's leadership, vision, and courage have been instrumental in shaping the organization's success, and her legacy will continue to inspire future generations of human rights advocates. Today, the RFK Human Rights organization remains one of the most respected and influential human rights organizations in the world, a fitting tribute to both Robert and Ethel Kennedy's relentless pursuit of justice.

Chapter Five

Key Battles: Ethel's Landmark Advocacy Campaigns

Ethel Kennedy's relentless pursuit of justice has left an indelible mark on the world of human rights advocacy. Born into privilege and married into the iconic Kennedy family, she could have easily remained in the background, content with the roles assigned to women of her status during her era. Yet, Ethel took a different path, driven by her personal losses and a profound sense of duty to champion the causes that her late husband, Robert F. Kennedy, held dear. As a widow and a mother of eleven, Ethel's activism became her own, built on a foundation of empathy for the oppressed and a tireless commitment to justice. Her involvement in landmark advocacy campaigns has made her one of the most formidable forces in human rights, not just in America, but around the world.

Ethel's journey as an advocate for justice was profoundly influenced by the political and social upheavals of the late 20th century. After her husband's assassination in 1968, Ethel found herself at a crossroads. The Kennedy legacy of service and justice had been shattered by violence. Yet, rather than retreating into grief, Ethel embraced Robert's ideals and made them her own. Her advocacy began as a continuation of Robert's work, but soon expanded into new areas that would shape her unique legacy. In particular, her support for Native American rights, the fight against apartheid in South Africa, and her advocacy for immigrants and refugees stand as testament to her enduring commitment to global justice.

One of Ethel's earliest and most impactful causes was the fight for Native American rights. Her deep involvement with the American Indian Movement (AIM) was born out of a growing awareness of the historic and ongoing injustices faced by Native American communities. At a time when Native American activism was gaining national attention, Ethel recognized the importance of using her platform to bring visibility to their struggles. The 1970s saw a series of high-profile protests by AIM, including the occupation of Alcatraz Island and the armed standoff at Wounded Knee, South Dakota. Ethel's public support for the movement brought national media attention to these events, as her status as a Kennedy made her a powerful ally in the fight for indigenous rights.

Ethel's involvement extended beyond mere endorsement; she made personal visits to Native American communities, meeting with activists and tribal leaders to better understand their plight. Her advocacy was instrumental in bringing about increased federal funding for Native American education, healthcare, and legal assistance. Ethel recognized that the injustices faced by Native Americans were not just historical grievances but present-day realities that demanded immediate action. She helped raise millions of dollars through the Robert F. Kennedy Human Rights Foundation for programs that supported Native American self-determination. Through her efforts, Ethel contributed to the passage of key legislation, including the Indian Self-Determination and Education Assistance Act of 1975, which granted greater autonomy to Native tribes. Her dedication to this cause remains one of the cornerstones of her advocacy work.

In the global arena, Ethel took a firm stand against apartheid, one of the most egregious systems of racial oppression in modern history. South Africa's apartheid regime, which institutionalized racial segregation and disenfranchisement of the Black majority, drew widespread international condemnation. Yet, for years, many Western governments and corporations maintained economic ties with the apartheid regime, turning a blind eye to the suffering it caused. Ethel, however, was unwavering in her opposition. She saw the fight against apartheid as a moral imperative and took a leadership role in galvanizing public opinion against the regime.

Her efforts included hosting high-profile fundraisers and public events to raise awareness about apartheid and the need for economic sanctions against South Africa. Ethel frequently spoke out in favor of divestment campaigns, which called on universities, corporations, and governments to pull their investments from companies doing business with the apartheid regime. Her activism played a crucial role in the broader movement that eventually led to widespread sanctions against South Africa, weakening the regime's financial base and contributing to its eventual collapse.

In 1985, Ethel took her activism a step further when she led a delegation of human rights advocates to South Africa, despite the government's attempts to block her entry. While in South Africa, she met with anti-apartheid activists, including Desmond Tutu and members of the African National Congress (ANC), who were fighting against the apartheid regime. Ethel's visit received significant international media coverage, helping to spotlight the brutality of apartheid and further galvanizing global opposition. Her visit was a powerful symbol of solidarity with the oppressed, and it demonstrated her willingness to put herself at the forefront of the struggle for justice.

As apartheid crumbled and South Africa transitioned to democracy, Ethel continued to be an outspoken advocate for reconciliation and justice. She worked closely with organizations like the Truth and Reconciliation Commission, which sought to address the crimes of the apartheid era and foster healing in the deeply divided nation. Ethel's commitment to South Africa's fight for justice did not end with the fall of apartheid; she remained engaged in the country's efforts to build a fairer and more equitable society in the years that followed.

Ethel's advocacy also extended to one of the most pressing global issues of our time: immigration and refugee rights. Her compassion for displaced populations was deeply personal, rooted in her Catholic faith and the values of service and justice that defined her family's legacy. Ethel recognized the humanitarian crisis facing refugees fleeing war, persecution, and poverty in various parts of the world. She became a vocal advocate for humane immigration policies and a critic of government actions that criminalized or marginalized refugees and immigrants.

In the 1980s and 1990s, Ethel's work with the Robert F. Kennedy Human Rights Foundation focused on providing legal assistance to asylum seekers and refugees. The foundation played a pivotal role in cases where refugees were being unlawfully detained or deported. Ethel's involvement helped to secure the release of several political prisoners and refugees who had been wrongly imprisoned or denied asylum. Her advocacy was not limited to legal battles, however; she also worked to raise awareness about the root causes of the refugee crisis, including conflict, economic inequality, and environmental degradation.

Ethel was particularly vocal about the treatment of Central American refugees fleeing civil wars in countries like El Salvador and Guatemala. She condemned U.S. policies that supported oppressive regimes in the region and advocated for a more compassionate approach to immigration. Her work helped to shift public opinion on immigration and contributed to the eventual passage of more humane immigration policies, including the 1986 Immigration Reform and Control Act, which provided a pathway to citizenship for millions of undocumented immigrants.

Ethel's advocacy for immigrant rights continued well into the 21st century. She remained a fierce critic of policies that sought to separate families at the border, detain children in inhumane conditions, or deport refugees to countries where they faced certain danger. Her voice was a constant reminder that the fight for human rights does not stop at national borders and that justice must be extended to all people, regardless of their country of origin.

Throughout her decades of activism, Ethel Kennedy's relentless pursuit of justice has been characterized by her ability to see beyond individual causes and recognize the interconnectedness of all struggles for human rights. Whether fighting for the rights of Native Americans, standing against apartheid, or advocating for immigrants and refugees, Ethel's work has always been rooted in a profound belief in the dignity of all human beings. She has used her platform to amplify the voices of the oppressed, and her advocacy has had a lasting impact on the global fight for justice.

Chapter Six

Legal Justice: Her Impact in the Courtroom

Ethel Kennedy's relentless pursuit of justice is a testament to her unwavering commitment to human rights and the legal system's role in upholding them. Throughout her life, she has championed the underprivileged, the marginalized, and those denied the basic protections of the law. While much of her advocacy has taken place in public forums and global campaigns, one of the most significant areas of her impact has been in the courtroom. Her work in supporting legal efforts to defend the wrongfully accused, advocating for the abolition of the death penalty, and ensuring that human rights are upheld in legal systems across the world has made her a powerful figure in the fight for justice.

Ethel Kennedy's courtroom impact began with her deep understanding of how the law can be a tool of both oppression and liberation. She recognized that, while legal systems are meant to serve justice, they often fail the most vulnerable. Her advocacy was not just about promoting laws that align with human rights but about ensuring that these laws are applied fairly and equitably. This sense of purpose drove her to become an influential voice in various legal battles, particularly in supporting organizations that worked to overturn wrongful convictions and reform criminal justice systems.

One of the most notable aspects of Ethel Kennedy's legal activism was her support for the

Innocence Project, a legal organization dedicated to exonerating the wrongfully convicted through DNA evidence. Ethel understood that wrongful convictions not only ruin the lives of innocent individuals but also undermine public trust in the legal system. Her involvement with the Innocence Project reflected her belief that no justice could be served if innocent people languished in prisons. Through her advocacy and financial support, she helped the organization gain traction in overturning high-profile wrongful convictions, shining a light on the flaws in the justice system, particularly when it came to marginalized communities.

Ethel's commitment to this cause was deeply personal. Having witnessed the political assassinations of her husband, Robert F. Kennedy, and his brother, President John F.

Kennedy, she understood the fragility of life and the importance of justice. However, her activism was not driven by revenge or anger but by a profound belief in the need for a fair and impartial legal system. Her advocacy efforts helped amplify the stories of those wrongfully accused, bringing national attention to issues of racial and socio-economic biases that contribute to wrongful convictions. Her tireless work alongside legal teams ensured that innocent individuals had access to the legal resources they needed, often resulting in exonerations that changed lives.

Beyond her support for the wrongfully accused, Ethel Kennedy became a formidable opponent of the death penalty. Her opposition to capital punishment was rooted in her deep religious faith and her belief in the sanctity of life. Ethel viewed the death penalty as a cruel and irreversible punishment that disproportionately affected the poor and people of color. She believed that the justice system, prone to human error, should not wield the power to take life, especially when the possibility of wrongful convictions existed.

Ethel's fight against the death penalty placed her at the forefront of national and international movements to abolish capital punishment. She worked with organizations such as the Death Penalty Information Center and Amnesty International to raise awareness about the flaws in the system, particularly the way in which capital punishment was applied unevenly across different racial and socio-economic groups. Ethel was deeply involved in advocacy efforts that highlighted the high rate of wrongful convictions in death row cases, reinforcing the need for systemic reform. Her influence was felt in both legal and public spheres, where she used her platform to speak out against the injustices inherent in the death penalty system.

Ethel's work was not just limited to the United States. Her influence extended to international human rights law, where she used her status and connections to advocate for justice in countries plagued by human rights abuses. She played an instrumental role in bringing attention to cases of political prisoners and human rights violations in countries such as South Africa, Chile, and the Philippines. Through her foundation, the Robert F. Kennedy Human Rights organization, she supported legal efforts to protect human rights defenders, ensuring they had access to legal representation in hostile environments. Ethel believed that the fight for justice could not be confined to national borders. Human rights were universal, and legal systems worldwide had to be held accountable.

Her impact on international law was particularly significant during the apartheid era in South Africa. Ethel was an outspoken critic of the South African government's use of the legal system to perpetuate racial segregation and oppression. She supported legal teams that fought for the release of political prisoners, including Nelson Mandela, and worked tirelessly to bring international attention to the legal injustices faced by black South Africans. Her involvement in this cause went beyond mere advocacy; she lobbied world leaders, spoke at international forums, and organized legal support for those fighting apartheid. Her work contributed to the eventual dismantling of apartheid, proving once again that the legal system could be a powerful tool for justice when wielded correctly.

Ethel Kennedy's legal impact also involved her efforts to ensure human rights were respected in American courts. She supported landmark cases that advanced civil rights, particularly those related to racial and gender equality. Ethel believed that the legal system should serve as a vehicle for social change and that the courts could play a pivotal role in advancing justice for marginalized communities. Her support for civil rights cases reflected her deep-seated belief in equality and fairness, values that had been instilled in her from a young age and were reinforced during her marriage to Robert

Kennedy, who himself was a champion of civil rights.

One of the most significant aspects of Ethel's legal advocacy was her ability to mobilize public opinion around key legal issues. She understood that legal battles could not be fought in the courtroom alone; they needed public support to bring about lasting change. Ethel was a master at using media and public forums to raise awareness about legal injustices. Her speeches, interviews, and public appearances often highlighted the importance of legal reform, urging Americans to take a stand against injustice. Whether it was fighting for the wrongfully accused, advocating against the death penalty, or supporting international human rights efforts, Ethel knew how to galvanize public support and create momentum for change.

Her legal impact has left an enduring legacy that continues to inspire human rights activists, lawyers, and advocates today. Ethel Kennedy's work in the courtroom, whether directly or through her support of legal teams, has resulted in tangible victories for human rights. She has shown that the law, when applied fairly, can be a powerful force for good, but when it fails, it must be challenged. Her relentless pursuit of justice, even in the face of adversity, has reshaped the legal landscape and brought attention to issues that had long been ignored or suppressed.

Chapter Seven

A Family Affair: Inspiring the Next Generation

Ethel Kennedy, a woman defined by both immense personal tragedy and remarkable resilience, stands as a testament to the indomitable spirit of activism. Throughout her life, she not only fought for justice but also sowed the seeds of advocacy in her family, ensuring that her legacy would transcend generations. The Kennedy name, synonymous with public service, owes much to her tireless commitment to human rights and social justice. Ethel's ability to inspire her children and future generations to take up the mantle of activism is one of her most enduring contributions, one that continues to shape the social and political landscape.

The story of Ethel Kennedy is not just one of a grieving widow carrying forward her husband's vision. It is also the story of a matriarch who profoundly influenced her children to follow in her footsteps, blending personal responsibility with public duty. After the assassination of her husband, Robert F. Kennedy, in 1968, Ethel was thrust into a role that demanded both resilience and leadership. Her home became a center for advocacy, a place where justice and human rights were not abstract concepts but living values. Her children, many of whom were still young at the time of RFK's death, grew up immersed in a world where action, not silence, was the response to injustice.

Ethel's approach to parenting was a reflection of her commitment to activism. She instilled in her children a deep sense of responsibility, not only to their family's legacy but also to the world around them. The Kennedy household was not one of luxury and privilege devoid of consequence; it was a place where service to others was paramount. Ethel made it clear that the Kennedy name carried weight and with it came the expectation of service and advocacy. Her children were not raised as mere heirs to a political dynasty but as individuals with their own agency, capable of making a difference in the world.

Central to Ethel's influence on her children was her unyielding commitment to human rights. Whether it was advocating for civil rights, supporting anti-apartheid movements, or championing indigenous rights, Ethel ensured that her children understood the importance of fighting for those without a voice. Her belief in the power of action was contagious, and it became the foundation upon which many of her children built their lives. Through conversations at the dinner table, family discussions on global issues, and the hands-on involvement in her many causes, Ethel ingrained in her children a sense of urgency when it came to confronting social injustice.

One of the most notable examples of Ethel's influence is seen in her son Robert F. Kennedy Jr., who has followed in his mother's footsteps as a staunch advocate for environmental justice. RFK Jr. has made it his life's mission to fight for the protection of natural resources and combat corporate greed that threatens ecosystems and marginalized communities. His dedication to environmental advocacy can be traced back to the values instilled in him by Ethel, who herself was passionate about safeguarding the earth for future generations. Ethel's commitment to social justice was holistic, encompassing both the rights of people and the preservation of the environment they inhabit. This belief was passed on to her children, especially RFK Jr., whose work has had a profound impact on environmental policy.

In addition to RFK Jr., Ethel's other children have also made significant contributions to the world of public service and advocacy. Kerry Kennedy, for instance, has been at the forefront of the human rights movement for decades. As the president of Robert F. Kennedy Human Rights, the organization founded to honor her father's legacy, Kerry has worked tirelessly to promote social justice and human rights across the globe. Under her leadership, the organization has expanded its reach, advocating for issues ranging from criminal justice reform to the rights of indigenous peoples. Like her mother, Kerry possesses an unwavering commitment to justice, and much of her work reflects the same passion for defending the disenfranchised that Ethel exemplified throughout her life.

Ethel's influence extended beyond her immediate children to the broader Kennedy family as well. The Kennedy cousins, inspired by their aunts, uncles, and grandparents, have continued the family tradition of public service. Joe Kennedy III, grandson of Robert and Ethel Kennedy, has carried on the family's legacy through his work as a U.S. Congressman and his dedication to progressive causes. His advocacy for healthcare reform, economic justice, and civil rights mirrors the values that Ethel instilled in her family. Even in the face of political opposition, Joe Kennedy III, like his relatives before him, remains steadfast in his commitment to justice and equity.

But Ethel's impact was not solely based on political careers or public office. Her influence permeated the everyday lives of her children and grandchildren, encouraging them to live with purpose and a sense of responsibility toward others. Many of the Kennedys have dedicated their time to charitable organizations, human rights work, and community activism. Whether through direct political action or quieter, behind-the-scenes work, Ethel's children have embraced the belief that their privilege obligates them to serve others. This ethos of giving back is perhaps one of Ethel's greatest legacies.

In the broader sense, Ethel Kennedy's fight for justice has had a ripple effect, inspiring not just her family but countless individuals who have been touched by her work and the work of her children. The RFK Human Rights organization, in particular, serves as a beacon of hope for activists and advocates worldwide. Under the leadership of Ethel and her children, the organization has grown into a formidable force in the global fight for justice. Through programs that promote human rights education, provide legal aid to those wrongfully convicted, and support activists on the frontlines of change, the RFK Human Rights foundation reflects Ethel's vision of a more just and equitable world.

What makes Ethel's legacy even more remarkable is her ability to adapt to the changing times. As new challenges emerged in the fight for human rights, Ethel's influence remained relevant. She has inspired her children to tackle modern-day issues such as climate change, LGBTQ+ rights, and economic inequality, ensuring that the fight for justice evolves to meet the needs of the current generation. This adaptability is one of the hallmarks of Ethel's legacy, allowing the Kennedy family to continue leading in areas of advocacy that resonate with contemporary social movements.

In the final analysis, Ethel Kennedy's relentless pursuit of justice has not only shaped the lives of her children but has also left an indelible mark on the world. Her children and grandchildren, inspired by her example, have carried forward the torch of activism, each in their unique way contributing to the fight for a more just and humane society. The Kennedy family remains a symbol of public service, not because of the wealth or power associated with their name, but because of the values of compassion, justice, and advocacy that Ethel so fervently embodied. Her fight for human rights was never just about her; it was about empowering those around her, especially her children, to carry on the mission of making the world a better place.

Chapter Eight

Legacy of Courage: The Enduring Impact of Ethel Kennedy's Work

Ethel Kennedy's relentless pursuit of justice and human rights has left an indelible mark on the world. For decades, she has been a formidable force in the fight for equality, human dignity, and social reform. Her work has spanned continents and causes, from advocating for the oppressed in distant lands to championing civil rights within the United States. Ethel's life has been shaped by both personal tragedy and an unwavering determination to continue the legacy of her late husband, Robert F. Kennedy. But her story is more than just an extension of his; it is one of a woman who found her own voice, her own mission, and who became a leader in her own right.

Ethel's activism was born from her profound sense of responsibility to carry forward the ideals of her husband. After Robert's assassination in 1968, she could have retreated into grief, but instead, she chose action. She refused to let his dreams die with him. In many ways, her journey was a testament to resilience. The strength she exhibited in the face of unimaginable loss became the foundation of her life's work. Ethel Kennedy's legacy is not just one of surviving tragedy but of transforming it into a powerful engine for change.

One of the most significant aspects of Ethel's enduring legacy is the founding of the Robert F. Kennedy Human Rights organization.

Established in 1968, shortly after her husband's death, the foundation became a powerful platform for promoting justice and human rights across the globe. Ethel was not content with passive charity work or simple commemoration; she aimed for tangible, transformative change. Under her leadership, the foundation grew into one of the most influential human rights organizations in the world, tackling issues as diverse as political persecution, civil rights violations, and social inequality. The organization became a beacon of hope for many oppressed communities, offering legal aid, raising awareness, and pushing for policy reforms.

Ethel's work took her to some of the most dangerous and forgotten corners of the world. Whether it was addressing human rights abuses in Latin America, fighting apartheid in South Africa, or advocating for indigenous rights in the United States, Ethel never hesitated to use her influence to draw attention to the plight of the marginalized. Her advocacy was not limited to the high-profile causes that often captured media attention. Instead, she delved into complex, less visible issues, proving her commitment to justice was far from superficial. Ethel saw the world through a moral lens that left no room for compromise on human dignity. This unyielding stance is one of the key reasons her legacy remains so potent today.

Her impact on the global stage was profound. In the 1980s, Ethel Kennedy became a vocal critic of apartheid, lending her voice and resources to the international movement against South Africa's racist regime. Her efforts helped galvanize public opinion in the United States and contributed to the mounting pressure on the U.S. government to impose sanctions on South Africa. Her stance against apartheid was not just political; it was deeply personal. Ethel's belief in equality and human dignity meant that she saw the South African struggle as a universal fight for justice. Her support for Nelson Mandela and other anti-apartheid leaders is well-documented, and her advocacy played a crucial role in keeping the issue at the forefront of international discussions.

In addition to her work on international issues, Ethel was a steadfast advocate for civil rights within the United States. She actively supported the Civil Rights Movement in the 1960s and continued to push for racial equality throughout her life. Her work with the Robert F. Kennedy

Human Rights organization focused on ending racial discrimination in the U.S. criminal justice system. Ethel was particularly passionate about reforming the death penalty, which she saw as an affront to human rights. Her advocacy in this area extended beyond the courtroom. She worked tirelessly to raise awareness of wrongful convictions and the systemic racism that often influenced death penalty cases. Her efforts have led to the exoneration of numerous individuals who were wrongly convicted, and her fight continues to inspire today's activists working toward criminal justice reform.

Ethel's commitment to justice was not confined to the legal or political spheres. She was also deeply invested in improving the lives of children and families, particularly those affected by poverty. She believed that true justice required addressing the root causes of inequality, and poverty was at the heart of many of the world's injustices. Through the Robert F. Kennedy Human Rights organization and other philanthropic efforts, Ethel worked to create educational opportunities for disadvantaged children, improve access to healthcare, and provide resources for struggling families. She understood that systemic change required not only policy reforms but also direct action to improve people's daily lives.

Perhaps one of the most inspiring aspects of Ethel Kennedy's legacy is her ability to galvanize others. She was not content with simply doing the work herself; she wanted to inspire others to join the fight. Ethel recognized the power of collective action and believed that lasting change could only come through sustained, grassroots efforts. She nurtured a generation of human rights advocates, many of whom continue to lead critical battles for justice today. Her influence extended far beyond the walls of the Kennedy family's philanthropic empire. Ethel's mentorship and leadership have inspired countless individuals to dedicate their lives to fighting for the rights of the oppressed.

Her personal courage has been a defining characteristic of her public life. Ethel Kennedy faced numerous threats and challenges throughout her career as an advocate. From receiving death threats during her involvement in civil rights campaigns to enduring public scrutiny, she never wavered in her commitment to her causes. Her tenacity in the face of adversity became a hallmark of her leadership. Ethel's willingness to stand up to powerful interests, whether they were governments, corporations, or social institutions, set her apart as a true leader in the fight for justice.

Ethel's story is not only one of activism but of enduring influence. The Robert F. Kennedy Human Rights organization remains a powerful force for good in the world today, continuing to tackle issues ranging from climate justice to LGBTQ+ rights. Ethel's children and grandchildren have followed in her footsteps, taking up the mantle of advocacy and continuing to push for social change. This multi-generational commitment to justice is perhaps one of her greatest legacies. Ethel understood that the fight for human rights was never-ending and that each generation must take up the challenge to make the world a more just and equitable place.

In recent years, Ethel's work has been recognized with numerous awards and honors, but perhaps the greatest tribute to her legacy is the ongoing impact of the causes she championed. The movements she helped create, the lives she touched, and the injustices she helped expose have left an indelible mark on society. Her work has inspired countless others to take action, and her legacy continues to be a driving force for those who believe in the power of justice and human rights.

www.ingramcontent.com/pod-product-compliance
Lightning Source LLC
Chambersburg PA
CBHW072030150726
47999CB00002B/839